Water Music

William Doreski

Cyberwit.net
HIG 45 Kaushambi Kunj, Kalindipuram
Allahabad - 211011 (U.P.) India
http://www.cyberwit.net
Tel: +(91) 9415091004 +(91) (532) 2552257
E-mail: info@cyberwit.net

Printed at Repro India Limited.

In Memory of Sam Cornish

These poems, sometimes in different versions, have appeared in *Axolotl, Azure, Chiron Review, The Curator, Dead Snakes, Dryland, 805 Literary and Arts Journal, Fire Tetrahedron, Former People, FriGG, Gravel, Logophilia, Lummox, Magnolia Review, Modern Poetry Quarterly Review, Mudfish, Potato Eyes, Screech Owl, Sediments, Smokey Blue, THAT Literary Review*, and *Yellow Medicine*. Many thanks to the editors of these journals.

Contents

Learning from Picasso

You're curating late Picasso
at the Museum of Fine Arts.
Because the paintings masticate
their subjects to pulpy shards
you've inspired yourself to replace
your teeth with plastic, ceramic,
or possibly stainless steel.

The show opens with slop and slur
of cocktails and hors d'oeuvres. Thick
and arrogant with power, donors
pose for *Globe* photographers
while the aesthetes like me wring
our hands and hang out as far
from the bar as possible. You stride

among the elite like police
on the beat. They haven't heard
your plan to replace your smile
with the most frightening dentures
you can find. But you believe
in art, not nature, and art speaks
the language of money, the one

global tongue. The thick people
crowd the bar, guzzling drinks
too volatile for people like me
to handle without fracturing
along predictable fault lines.

They all sport custom dental work
in the Carpenter Gothic style.

You want them to vomit dollars
right there on the marble tile.
underwriting future exhibits
Your hairdo bobs on the swells
as you cross the room to shake
my hand and hope I've enjoyed
the liquor and snacks. Your smile,

even with your familiar old teeth,
is a death trap. Once you shark yourself
with artificial choppers you'll ingest,
by default, everything around you,
learning from Picasso how
to render any subject foolish
for the sake of a higher cause.

For Joanne

Ten years old that afternoon
in the dingle, you kissed me
so hard my teeth hurt. We knew
more about nuclear fusion
in stars than about the bodies
we tried to mesh. The brook sighed
those elegant little water sighs
many mistake for human sighs.
This was long before parental deaths
left holes in the summer sky
through which entire galaxies fell
in a shower of nuclear sparks.
The vanilla flavor of your kisses
has lingered now for sixty years
although I wouldn't know you
if I passed you in the local mall.
The dingle still fumes this August
with deer flies bunching like fists.
Familiar rocks sport top hats of moss.
The two-inch depth of the brook
seems too fragile to have flowed
so long without drowning itself.
I find the grassy bank we lay on
with the imprint of our bodies
still visible. That raw Sunday
afternoon taught us nothing.
Stripping naked revealed no secrets
for overwrought fantasies to gnaw.
We rolled around for awhile

then splashed in the brook and dried
each other with our underwear.
Clammy and glad we dashed back
to the dead-end street you lived on.
The geometry of the houses
rebuked us, but we didn't care—
the gargling of the dingle brook
riper than the skins we bared.

Virtual and Virginal

Half-toppled, broken ten feet up,
a maple claws at the sky.
Still leafing, it doesn't yet know
how to die. A windless day,
yet the smooth weight of drizzle
tipped the balance. Nothing so trite
as a falling tree. Caught in the boughs
of its neighbors, it could maintain
that helpless posture for years.

Too late to get out the chainsaw
and help it fall in one clean chunk.
I stare up into writhing branches
and will myself into empathy.
Although too old to instruct
the cell phone generation I stand
upright through hour-long lectures,
insist on respectful decorum,
and question the digital sublime
at its binary root.

    School opens
Monday, after a rainy summer
of lost virginities and vomit
splotches on beachfront sidewalks.
Unlike my dazzled students
my view of the sea is so distant
it's hardly a mote in the eye.
Still, the scything hiss of breakers

fills one ear, while the other
catches snatches of conversation
as people chat on their cell phones
in languages I don't understand.

The Bridge at Trinquetaille

(Arles, 1888)

Long stone slabs, a flight of steps
leading from a roughly cobbled street.
Then a narrower stairway flanked
by thick concrete walls, twenty-six
risers to a modern steel bridge,
gray stringers trussed above
a swirl of white space. Figures,
van Gogh's usual stocky blobs,
muddle up and down and along
the bridge, their errands obscure,
undelineated. Only
a red protective wrapping
about a sprig of foreground sapling
violates the blue-green-gray
of the wholly architectural
composition. To live in so
rigid a scene would humble
the grossest of Christians. The cracked
eggshell of sky allows no god
to peer at the people hunching
along their determined routes.
Yet van Gogh drew this freehand,
and in the reckless execution
he allowed his composition
to escape him, slurring and flexing
and finally escaping into
the boughs of a tree barely glimpsed

beyond the arch on the right,
the only natural perspective.

Like Many Giant Footprints

You claim that despair stalks friends,
poaching in their teacups and slurring
their favorite words. The cold wind
tastes of stone. The post office
slumps on its foundations. Mail
from the last century still awaits
delivery, gummed flaps muttering.
Meanwhile the wind plunges and plunges
with the angst of dolphins hunted
to extinction. Shoppers toting bags

of primary goods recall
their childhoods in other nations,
even if born here in a welter
of sticky limbs. You want to warn them
that when the snowdrifts melt
certain clues will emerge. Maybe
diamond tiaras stolen too late
to catch the evening news. Maybe
cigar butts that crawled from Cuba
to subvert fat-headed old men

who always vote Republican.
The newly kindled sunlight fails
to deter the wind from prying
into our open pores and scalding
tears we've saved for our funerals.
But you laugh your rhinestone laugh
and note that wherever volcanoes

burst the earth new opportunities
follow, like many giant footprints
leading to the planet's far edge.

Brooklyn Ferry, a Ghost Story

After taking my daily pills
I fall from the ferry and drown.
The Brooklyn Ferry, Whitman's beard

plowing the river in sparkles
of sun. The engine smuts
the yellow sky with coal smoke.

The passengers in smelly woolens
clump like clots of moss on rock.
Manhattan without skyscrapers

exudes a rattle of carts, drays,
and wagons. Whitman tosses
a life preserver to save me,

but I'm so old and stony I sink
with pitiless glee to the bottom.
The mud engorges me. I'm fish

food before I've finished drowning.
This isn't funny, but the crowd
on the ferry laughs a huge gray

nineteenth century laugh designed
to drive its victims insane.
I can hear it while the fish nose

and nibble and my lungs pump
like sump pumps and the fresh
but oily water mingles with salt

to brew my future in the stars.
The Brooklyn Ferry hasn't run
since John and Washington Roebling

completed their gothic bridge
with diagonal harp-strung cables
and walkway down the center.

I'm walking that walkway right now.
I wave at the crowd of ghosts
on the ghost ferry steaming across

the East River with coal smoke
the color of Whitman's beard
and a school of grim suicides

paddling in its wake, every one
determined to reach Manhattan
before it finally drifts away.

Clay-Colored

Miranda steals shiny trinkets
from the elderly and pawns them.
When I reach into her bosom

and extract my Timex watch
her innocence recedes like a tide.
A crowd gathers. Miranda

in a pique of fury undresses
completely, shedding jewelry,
pill boxes, lighters, money clips,

and enough watches to daunt
every time zone on the planet.
Naked, she glowers with fission.

Her jaws creak as if a great scream
has fossilized deep inside her.
The crowd murmurs with pity

and glowers at me, so I leave
with my watch ticking on my wrist
and a vision of Miranda's

clay-colored body brimming.
The rest of the day discolors
like an old bruise. The post office

coughs up bills and circulars.
The coffee shop's too busy
to prepare my mocha latte

with the right shade of chocolate.
The market offers weird cuts of beef
crudely torn from celestial cows.

Miranda will probably stalk
and knife me in my sleep;
and when police find my watch

ticking in her bosom she'll feign
such guilt they'll feel ashamed,
and neglect to arrest her.

From Bartlett's Quotations

Reading from *Bartlett's Quotations*
aloud in the coffee shop
you smother all conversations

and frustrate people on cell phones
chatting about private matters
they wish to expose to the world.

"A stitch in time saves nothing,"
you read. "A fool and his bladder
are soon parted." "Early to bed,

better off dead." "Red sky at dusk,
your sailboat will rust." Which edition
of Bartlett's are you quoting?

Your expression clouds. Customers
shrug into their coats and depart.
The coffee smells of formaldehyde.

Far beneath us a volcano
is brewing, its evil temper
a dream of molten crystals.

Long after we're gone it will surge
like a boil and pop. The lava
will erase this civilization

and cool into layers of basalt
too black to let warmth or light escape
to encourage new evolutions.

Only your ghost will linger,
mouthing new crops of quotations
but no longer sounding them.

At last you close your book and stare
into your coffee cup, exhausted
by scholarly exertion. I snatch

the book and flip through it.
Every page is blank. Outside,
a snow shower blinds the parking lot

with a dense gray scrim, and silence
maps its heavy old footfall
from here to there and back again.

The Lobotomizing Angel

My journals shredded overnight,
refuting every hard-earned word.
The computer's cyclops eye self
blinded, erasing the only
locally competitive intellect.
Shelves of books have toppled.

When I paw through their pages
each is blank. War and politics
flashed and thundered after midnight.
Yet the scribbles in my journals
and the text painfully typed
into my computer said nothing

about healing the rasp of bone
on bone, metal on bedrock.
I didn't name names except those
Adam refused to whisper to Eve.
But the lobotomizing angel
has flitted through my house

to deny my lifetime of work
a hearing. I sweep up the scraps
of journal and toss the junk
computer into a trash bag
for a trip to the landfill. Maybe
after a while the text will return

to those formerly printed books.
Snowdrifts thaw slowly in weak
March sun. The longest month
of the year. Or so I scrawled
in one of those vandalized journals,
or maybe typed on the laptop

that no longer possesses a mind.
Self-rebuttal's out of fashion—
nuclear war glooms the horizon,
and the chat of birds at the feeders
effects a grammar too vivid
for any journal to contain.

The Film Version

In the film version I tote
five gallons of gasoline
to the entry of the institute

where our baby died and you
remain imprisoned. The sky
gloats in pink marbled textures.

Anonymous music resounds.
Security guards equipped
with tasers stare me down.

But they're behind glass doors,
so I pour the gas, splashing it
under the door. They step back,

paw at their radios. I snap
a match and the screen goes blank.
The audience groans. The film

has ended, the smut of popcorn
crunching underfoot. You grip
my arm in fear. Can we face

the summer evening having spent
twenty dollars on tickets
when we knew we'd failed to film

a proper heroic ending?
What if the dispersing audience
recognizes us from the screen?

The parking lot's the Black Sea,
deep and treacherous. We splash
through the shallows to our car.

In the air conditioned dark
we agree to let the baby
go unnamed forever, the film

too merciful to show the corpse
and your face without thick makeup
too blank to show its disgrace.

Between Germany and Poland

The gap between Germany
and Poland is no wider
than the part in your hair. Rain sifts
fact from fiction. You linger
over coffee brewed to rival
jet fuel. You insist that Google
Maps no longer include
townships abandoned when cops
smashed down the doors to nab
anyone who voted Democrat.
You claim that the waiter who served
your bowl of mussels wore
spywear and looked sideways to catch
your profile cast in shadow.
I argue over my salad
that coefficients don't apply
to factors based on the human.
You, with more serious math,
have cubed the effects of poverty
squared by terror. I can't count
that high. Not enough fingers
and toes. Puddles in the street catch
glimpses of another world
and display them to pedestrians
splashing to the nearest bar.
We snuggle into our booth
and pretend the Second World War
doesn't apply to us. The waiter
minces to our table and snatches

your credit card, presses it
to his heart. More black coffee
would cure us of the trembling
that always occurs at the border
between German and Poland—
the grumble of tanks displaced
by the angst of digestion,
the overcast of your gaze.

Borneo Neighbors England

The world has remapped itself
so Borneo neighbors England.
We borrow a sailboat in Dover
and point the bow southeast

where Calais used to cower
around its geometric harbor.
The Chunnel goes nowhere now.
France has moved south of Africa,

and Africa has displaced Brazil.
A hundred miles to Bintulu.
Although neither of us can sail,
we voyage there without incident.

We hike from there to the heart
of Borneo, where two hundred
species of bats descend
and tangle in our hair. You scream

that scream made famous on film
and I faint in a dozen shades
of cerulean. Langurs,
slow lorises, gibbons inspect us

as we lie on the jungle floor
and become encrusted with ants
as long and thick as fountain pens.
We rise abruptly and scatter

pangolins and flying squirrels
as dawn light flushes the bats.
Civets and bearcats nose about
and avoid us. After three weeks

of slogging through our own sweat
we emerge in Paris and agree
that the world hasn't shifted
its continents after all, that

Borneo was a state of mind
we embraced for reasons too shy
to expose to each other. Lazing
in a Montparnasse café we blame

ourselves in shadowy tones,
and agree that the orangutans
that have followed us to the city
aren't ancestors, only friends.

On the Way to Jericho

On the way to Jericho we pause
in a fuzzy little village wrought
of driftwood and yellow brick.
Citizens shaped like teapots prowl
shops peddling yard goods, T-shirts,
and cookware. The houses smile
through a grit of coal dust. Railroads
mate in the center of town. A church
glooms over a rusty skating pond
edged with ice. Christmas is creeping
through the shrubbery. Ribbons flop
on red enameled doors. Blue lights
edge the town hall, a confection
of belated Queen Anne brickwork.
You want a cup of cocoa. I need
a dose of rum to ease the growling
of organs for which I've no respect.
A tavern beckons with a jukebox
coughing up Bob Dylan carols.

Jericho's only another two
or three hundred miles. We'll sleep
in the car. We won't risk the inn
here, a ghostly purple sheen
flashing in the dusky windows.
You say the cocoa tastes earthy,
but you drink it down anyway.
The rum aches like transfusion
and solves my immediate needs.

When we step outside, the village
looks riper, homier, and people
greet us by name. No need to drive
all the way to Jericho when stars
pepper the dying sky and a cottage
yawns to digest us, body and soul,
the dark rooms brimming with the cries
of our famous unborn children.

Your Libido

You worry that your libido
will detach on hot nights and prowl
half-abandoned neighborhoods
for men so addled by crack or speed

they'll mistake your ghostly excrescence
for the muse of their drug of choice.
You fear that in their attempts
to sexually master vacancies

between themselves and the rainbow
of your presence they'll employ
organs designed for other use
and destroy themselves in bloodbaths

the police won't try to explain.
Lightning sizzles in the north.
The river, dammed at its mouth,
reflects skyscrapers lit until dawn.

You lie awake with a volume
of Tolstoy, hoping your libido
will return without that vicious smile
that means it has killed again

without your permission. Later
over breakfast you'll confer
with a couple of yawning lawyers
who will deny your liability

by claiming that some insanities
shine like pyrites and confuse
even the wariest with fevers
not even Freud himself could tame.

The streets, glossy with last night's rain,
will greet you with the routine
of traffic, snarl of diesel buses,
and taxis gleaming like lilies.

You'll hulk in your office and deploy
functionaries to the world's end,
snuffling through useless memos
like a hound after truffles;

and when gasping and drooling
your libido returns you'll greet it
with a perfunctory handshake
and no invitation to sit.

The Last of the Argonauts

On the ferry to Crete I clutch
the bag of produce you gave me:
carrots, potatoes, turnips, kale.

I wanted mangoes, lemons, almonds,
but you thought I'd get scurvy
or rickets, thought an earth-taste

would preserve me. A raw little squall
of unseasonable April snow
dances across the deck. The ferry's

huge as a cruise ship. Afraid to fly
after that German pilot's suicide
in the Alps, taking a hundred

and fifty people with him, I stashed
my luggage in a locker, swallowed
the key. The thought of lemons

bitter enough to fell cities,
sweet enough to engender
empires richer than Persia's,

urged me to hike the backlands
of Crete and scout the ruins for clues
to antiquity's most famous nudes.

You waved and pretended to cry
as the ferry lurched out to sea,
carving the Aegean blue

into a thousand random gestures.
Hooting at tiny sailboats
it stifled the crudest sentiments.

So goodbye to you, and thanks
for the vegetables. One by one
I drop them overboard, marking

a sea-trail you can follow to Crete
to learn which stones to lick for moisture
and which I completely ingest.

The Difference that Clouds Make

I haven't showered for a week,
so in paper slippers I trek
half a mile to the bathhouse
and find an armless, legless man
shelved on a slippery tile ledge.
He appears asleep or dead,
so I step into the steamy rush
and scour myself silly and pink.
When I step out, the man's gray lips
wrestle as he tries to explain.
Combing my hair produces
bursts of electrostatic sparks.
Toweling my awkward torso
requires so much effort I fail
to focus on the man's whispers,
although I catch some phrases
like *green is the night* and *men
in helmets borne on steel.* Maybe
I should recognize the source
of these random quotations;
but although limbless the man
now waves ghostly arms and stands
on smoky full-length trousers.
Maybe he had simply folded
himself unnaturally compact.
Maybe he has regenerated
his limbs in the moist fungal air.
Maybe his spirit has assumed
the role his body used to play.

He mutters, *the difference that clouds
make over a town.* I shake
his misty ghost-hand to encourage
his attempt to materialize.
He almost musters a smile.
Then bulked in my terry bathrobe
I withdraw, scraping my slippers
along the gravel path outside,
back to my cabin where I pose
legless and armless in a mirror
that has never flattered me
and doesn't recall my name.

House-Sized Ice Floes

East of Brunswick, railroad tracks
crumble in rust. The next train
will derail in a huff of exhaust
and clatter of aimless wheels.
From the overpass I observe

rats bustling in a drainage ditch.
Food is always their purpose,
food to fatten themselves for winter,
food for litters of little pink rats
cuddled in nests beside the ditch.

I'm hitchhiking to the seashore
where I expect house-sized ice floes
to crumble up and shatter. Despite
the lack of snow-cover the cold
speaks with authority. Trees creak

in the wind. No Christmas shopping
this year, no one expecting
even the ghost of a greeting
from me. I could stand here for years
and no train would come along

to derail in a gust of drama.
That era has passed. The cackle
of birds in the colorless distance
suggests where the sea is thrashing
in Technicolor green, blue, gray.

I might be a month or so early
for ice floes, but learning the language
of creation requires me
to dip a hand in the icy brine
and consider where I came from.

Maybe like the *Titanic* I'll crash
on the ice and sink inside myself,
and the rusty old railroad tracks
like a sprig of broken syntax
will elongate into elegy.

The House You left in Poland

The house you left in Poland,
the one you painted socialist gray,
has become a nightclub. Neon
curlicues adorn a façade
of pink stucco. Couples shiver
with excitement as they enter,
certain the floor show will expose
their private desires and arouse
the most flattering little blushes.

I occupy a table for one.
A green drink smelts before me.
The air tastes of industry.
Everyone speaks Polish or French,
German, Czech, or Russian. Alone
in my language, I eat and drink
whatever the waiter selects.

The floor show, the really famous one,
begins. A judge in carmine robes
drools over a clutch of naked
and cringing miscreants, men
and women. A gallows looms.
The condemned sing a dolorous tune
to underscore their nakedness,
which sets the memory jangling.

Before the audience can focus
on this collective memory

the hanging occurs. The bodies jerk
and stiffen. It's all over,
it's real. Yet later I note
drinking at the bar two women
who were hanged, nicely clothed now
and chatting. And that waiter
also stood among the condemned,
his genitals drooping sadly.

You'd enjoy this nightclub although
you'd wish it were still your home
with that dull patina of Marxist
theory, the thick oak furniture
crouching in drawn-curtain dimness
around a vase of paper roses
like Neanderthals around a fire.

In Your Secular Majesty

A burnt-out apartment block
overlooks the bicyclist crushed
by a big truck at the corner
of Beacon. A crowd gathers,
but I dodge down the alley,
admiring the antique brickwork,
and emerge into dappled gray
with a view of glass skyscrapers
grinning with brutalist power.

I want to be urban enough
to accept the grid-plan of streets
as a natural excrescence.
I want the fatal traffic to stall
long enough for me to escape
into the lobby of the building
where your acolytes worship
with legally approved gestures
and conscience clear as isinglass.

You won't receive me in person,
but inflamed by that accident,
which I witnessed in full color,
I'm ripe enough to render blue
and black and red and all shades
between, like a painter obsessed
with a bowl of rotting fruit.

You'll read about the bicyclist
and respond in the cacophony
of tones I've willed you. But
that muck of prismatic angst
obscures the ignorance of machines,
the blunt force of skyscrapers,
the cringing of alleys hidden
behind nineteenth-century houses.

You in your secular majesty
perched in an upper-floor office
overlook nothing but a fog
of pearly yellow vapors
most people mistake for residue
of things we're afraid to say.

Second World War Still Unsolved

Even after severe bombing,
the wooden hangars stand unscathed.
Adolf Hitler himself, moustache
twitching, scampers from the dust-cloud,
runs for the woods. We stop and frisk him,
then let him go.

Let him go?
I scream in sleep and wake myself.
The silence mists with ghosts too faint
to assume much form. Six million
dead in the camps, surely another
six million on the Russian steppes.

Before I was born, they cried aloud,
naming the finest grains of sand
after themselves, naming molecules
after themselves, starving blades of grass
after themselves.

I heard those cries
linger in the roses and lilacs
my grandmother, considering
Poland's agony, planted.

Whitewashed fences, hand-mown lawns,
clapboard houses with coal-fired
hot-air furnaces. These I recall
from the Forties while Auschwitz sank

into itself, groaning with shame,
the pine forests choked and yellowed.

Now more than fifty years too late,
I dream the war from start to finish.
Germany's merely an airfield
down the street from America,
and our canvas airplanes bomb it
and rattle everyone's teeth.

Yet face to face with Hitler I looked
into his filmy green eyes (my
Hitler has green eyes) and let him go.

Maybe he's not the villain he was
half a century ago. Maybe
he's the kind of spirit one good sneeze
sends whimpering to hell.

The dark house sighs. The pinewoods
remember nothing of Poland,
the distance too weighty with crime
for their pollen to negotiate;

though often I wake all slick
with soot from crematoria
half a world and lifetime away
no matter how deliberately
or full of purpose I've slept.

Swimsuit Issue

Raking snow from the roof excites me.
The feel of that weight giving way
and the thunder of its plunge inflame
greater depth of feeling than the *Sports
Illustrated* swimsuit issue does.

But I've never been as expert
at reading those vinyl bodies
as men are supposed to be.
I'm better with snow-struck New England
woodlots, chickadees perking in shrubs,
and deer tracks hashmarked everywhere.

These scenes feel more like the flesh
of my flesh than do those overpaid,
surgically finished models glazed
with smiles that cut my fingers
as I turn the varnished pages.

I should have returned to Poland
and learned the language and taught
English to young people eager
for a larger grip on the world.
Strolling up Nowy Swiat I'd stop
at cafés and chat with poets
whose work reaches more people than
the swimsuit issue does.

     But stuck
in the dreary north country winter
I choose for amusement to rake
the snow from the roof and feel
and hear its dissolution in drifts
that resemble speech balloons
emanating from the recent dead.

I've never experienced winter
in Poland, but understand it's raw
with memories of the war, even
for those born long after. I too
remember the war, though born
six months after it ended.
I hear it in the thump of snow
heaping at my feet, and feel it
suffer as I drag the rake
across the shingles.

     And I almost
see it evade the memory
in the dazzle of the swimsuit
models, their tough Aryan poses,
gilded on tropical landscapes,
incapable of understanding
the snowy outlook I love.

Third-Degree Blue

When I greet you among gray streets
near Union or Madison Square
the glare will seem blue as the smoke
of burning documents—your passport,
for instance, the one from Poland
that for years you pinned to garments
close to your heart. The reveries
of late Eighties politics shaped
your winsome gaze to linger
on the bottomless desires of men
and women alike, appraising them
with a smile too fragile to challenge.

Today the various organs claim
private space in pale winter sun.
You slump in your lover's grasp
and dream of bathing in vodka
chilled to flatter your temperament.
You understand how deeply
hibernation plumbs the ego
even in a steam-heated city
coughing a hundred deaths a day.

The snow-blue sickens me now
that I'm old enough to read it.
How can you lie so peacefully
in such an oblique embrace?
Not that I could replace the lover
you worked so hard to earn. But only

you and I realize that Poland
exported a view of the Baltic
to vex our ancestral memories
by reminding us how badly
this third-degree blue can burn.

Life Studies

In Russia and Poland the snow
rests so firmly on the graves
of ancestors that it anchors me
to the sentiment of windy
treeless plains and war-rumpled cities
rebuilt in faceless concrete.

I've no desire to visit the slow
black rivers that brim to the Baltic
or Caspian Sea, but sometimes
I feel the current underfoot
as if I waded in the shallows
perhaps to net shiners for bait,
perhaps to wash vegetables to boil
for dinner after sweating all day
grinding the valves of a tractor
or welding a harrow cracked by stones.

I've nearly fallen headlong
into maps that show no details,
no villages, roads, or railways
where my ancestors stumbled and died.
Perhaps the villages go nameless,
their slat-sided houses too shy
to attract the census taker,
their churches too blunt and modest
to catch the eye of their orthodox
but urbane and preoccupied god.

In America, where Slavic names
still ring like counterfeit quarters,
no one believes that landscapes
as worn and blind as Russia's
belong on the same bold planet
as our familiar suburban glut.

Yet I feel them overlap,
the snow cover thickening
across the temperate zones, cities
like Boston and St. Petersburg
confounded in a tangle of streets,
the Urals and the Adirondacks
conforming to mutual templates.

Now every cell of my body
replicates exactly one
of my ancestors', every gene
from that vast uncatalogued pool
poses like the scream in Münch's painting—
flesh dramatized by entropy,
avenged by the failure of nations.

Water Music

A pure orange topknot of fire
caps a block of Second Avenue.
Gas-fed disaster shaped to fit
the urban imagination. Cries
of spectators drift for miles,
occluding skyscraper views,
souring the hot-dog vendors
and stifling art in museums.

You should be here reflecting
the flames with your elegance
while absorbing heat for the future.
The clash of chrome steel nozzle
and rubber slicker keeps firefighters
excited by their profession.
The grunt of diesels pumping
water into bottomless rage
expresses a sense of distance
we otherwise would relegate
to organs too vague to plumb.

You enjoy these visceral moments,
but the people hurt in the blast,
their blood-mucked faces brimming,
stare into their losses with sighs.
The stink of fire will ghost through
most of Manhattan by dusk.
All the way to Washington Heights
people will ask what's burning,

what has burned. With a clash
of brick and shattered beams, a façade
crumples into the avenue.

From your office you can see
that spring has arrived with flowers
in Washington Square; but here,
a few blocks east, tangles of hose
suggest a great uprooting,
while the aerial streams compose,
against smoke plume and sky,
water music more graceful
than Handel's, more purposeful
than anything money can buy.

Logging in Nesting Season

Even in stolid morning rain
the scream of a chipper persists.
Loggers devour the forest
despite the protests of phoebes
and wood thrush. Their songs

penetrate like wounds you scored
half a lifetime ago although
you sleep right through the clamor,
your face pressed into the pillow.
I should wake and trouble you

over the outrage of logging
in nesting season, but rain-smells
dull me into shades of gray
I otherwise wouldn't inhabit.
The lake puckers as if coughing up

thousands of fish. A lone canoe
prowls along the shoreline, probing
for bass in the misty shallows.
The prattle of a chainsaw drops
another big tree. The chipper

gnarls the limbs while a winch
hoists the trunk onto a skidder.
Whoever nested in that tree
mourns the loss of effort and eggs,
maybe the death of nestlings.

You can't sleep this away.
The ill music skids across the lake
to fester in the cusp of the ear.
You'd better get up and share
the overall aura of complaint.

The day progresses step by step
as if learning something. No one
learns, though, the cries of machines
fluted more subtly than birdsong
and more finely honed to kill.

Carnage Incarnate

In the lukewarm purple dark
on Main Street bar patrons
cluster and buzz on the sidewalk.
We shuffle along with shy
but absolute footfall and agree
that the spring horizon lengthens
as the gap between us widens.

Your car, parked by the theater,
glooms with inertia. The gloss
of its finish catches lamplight
preening in chemical tints,
We leave each other breathing
the collective urban bar-breath
and hope the police don't catch us
proceeding with uneasy thoughts.

My modest apartment sighs
with ghosts shaped like the pets
I lost in childhood. Goldfish,
a turtle, a plush green parakeet.
I slam the door hard enough
to chase them into dimensions
I don't have to brave in life.

The streetlight explores corners
of my rooms, places I never
go alone. I wish you could see

how dusty, how deeply un-
inhabited this space becomes
when I've stepped out for an evening.

No one's here to understand
why I should brave the brazen streets
where the laws of physics doom me
to encounter certain force-fields
that demagnetize and render me
harmless enough to pocket
and innocent enough to discard.

A Field Guide Just for You

Gone to the Dry Tortugas,
you've left a yellow residue
for dogs to sniff in wonder.

Two hundred species of birds
pause on their way to nesting grounds
in the US and Canada.

You peer at them through binoculars
assembled deep in Germany,
costing more than I make in a month.

The high polish of the lenses
guarantees that the rarest birds
will appear to you and you only.

I expect Instagram or Facebook
to flower with the photographs
with which you'll educate me

in the plumage of brilliant species
I've rarely dreamed of spotting.
I expect to learn that rails, egrets,

bitterns, short and long-billed dowitchers.
phalaropes and terns have adopted
and made you an honorary bird.

Moorhens, kestrels, coots, plovers,
whimbrels, curlews, sanderlings, stilts,
shoverels, gadwells, red knots.

They must love the glossy gaze
of your expensive optics,
the click of your digital shutter.

You and you alone deserve these birds;
and when they've all gone extinct
in the roar and tumble of your wake

you'll cry on my shoulder and leave
more of that yellow residue
that puzzles and sickens the dogs.

On the Dark Side of Our Mountain

Along the gravel back roads
abandoned apple orchards
scratch at the cloudy spring dusk.

We can't map these roads because
shadows drift from the forest
and claim the heavy stone walls

and crude foundations of farms
obsolete before the Civil War.
A few modern houses spiked

with satellite dishes and sporting
big glossy pickup trucks
invite us with barking dogs

to keep going until we reach
the nearest paved highway.
You suspect ambush everywhere,

fear that having entered this maze
we can't escape. The shadows
thicken like cooling fat.

Thunder barks atop the hills.
Taking turns driving your old
gray Corolla doesn't resolve

the landscape until we cross
the unused railroad and realize
the state road meanders parallel

to the track. Friendly contours
ensue, and a village we know
as personally as a handshake.

All this wanderlust only
a few miles from home. The hills
nod and a spark of lightning

celebrates our escape, the carcass
of a struck porcupine deflated
in post-winter roadside grit.

How Little Horsepower Required

My motorbike earns a hundred
miles per gallon, but has burned
that gallon, so I have to wheel it
to the gas station where thugs
in pickups laugh at me. The day
burns like the midnight lantern
in the brakeman's hand. May
has brought its graces to bear
on everyone, even the toughs
with their big surly trucks.
I pump my gallon and putter
into dimensions too specific
for large vehicles to enter.
The road narrows to a path
in the woods. Smooth, graveled,
it leads past witch hovels
and shacks featuring incest
among pale hairless families.
It leads to a scraggy orchard
where deer strip the blossoms
every spring. I park and lie down
in tick-littered grass and dream
of surf breaking on lonely beaches
the famous nudes avoid. The creak
of old trees in the breeze suggests
how far from home this dead-end
has taken me. A hundred miles
per gallon, and I've used up thirty.
Hope I'm not lost. A thrush song

more vivid than any I've heard
in years soars over the orchard.
I stagger to my feet and mount
my bike and rev the tiny engine.
Thirty miles here, thirty back,
refill the tank and dawdle home
without a story to tell, the gloom
of the forest still heavy on me;
the forty miles left in the tank
the ones that would've taken me
wherever desperation belongs.

Your Flamingo Dance

In the new hotel in Hartford
in the most private of suites
you perform your flamingo dance

so adroitly that I explode
in a thousand shades of vermilion.
You learned flamingo in Florida,

where the creatures flock en masse.
Because their pink excites the roots
of your red hair you choreographed

steps no woman has ever stepped
before, tallowing long strides
across a Wagnerian stage

set in a mental Everglades
you enflame with candid style.
The hotel quivers with delight,

cheap artworks tumbling face-down
in homage, the beds quivering
with ghostly orgasm, the lobby

sofas crawling to the street to howl
at the flamingo-pink dawn.
The old hotel couldn't withstand

this muscular dance. The walls
would have bowed outward, nails
would spring from the studs, and souls

would perish in the sudden collapse.
I'm so glad you phoned me
after many years of erasure

to enact this primal display.
I'm to picture you feathered
and snake-necked, a beak probing

for manna, strut-legs bracing
against the threat of hurricane.
But naked and shining like metal

you still brazen entire worlds
in which actual flamingoes
have yet to evolve, the depth

of the marshlands still unplumbed
and the human parts of you
too smooth for others to grasp.

Quatrains for the First of May

You associate our favorite
sparkling water with yeast
sandwiches made by your mother
back home on the reservation.

I prefer the taste of warm brick
from the ruined mill building
by the river where we swam
naked right after the war.

Last night the Witches' Sabbath
again sealed your pact with Satan,
whose hot breath lingers long after
his departure in sly hosannas.

You always think that witchcraft
strong enough to topple buildings
can solve the latest mysteries
with dainty forensic spells.

You believe that the snoring of birds
in the earliest hours completes
song cycles that nature ordains
to consecrate favored landscapes.

I believe that nesting herons
in the marsh beyond the quarry
converse in a language too ripe
for even your ancestors to parse.

I also believe that the yeast
your mother fed you swelled your ego
to upholster your bony torso
against the ogling of men like me.

Yet the taste of sun-struck brick
from a structure toppled by fire
a lifetime before we were born
lingers longer than your kisses.

Maybe we should refine ourselves
to better conform to each other
before peepers finish mating
and the season eludes our grasp.